Contents

"You can measure the health of a city by the vitality and energy of its streets and public open spaces."
—WILLIAM H. WHYTE

Introduction

THE ULI URBAN OPEN SPACE AWARD celebrates and promotes vibrant, successful urban open spaces by recognizing and honoring outstanding examples of public destinations that enrich and revitalize the surrounding community.

Urban open spaces have a fundamentally transformative impact on the built environment. Cities' lasting success typically correlates with the value that open space provides as a means of leveraging economic growth and revitalization, as well as improving the quality of life for the growing urban population. These projects are spaces that we gravitate to—spaces where we share time with family and friends, interact with strangers, and relax in an urban setting that strengthens our ties to the community.

In 2009, the Urban Land Institute created and initially funded the award thanks to the vision of and a generous gift from Amanda Burden, then commissioner of the New York City Department of City Planning. She used the prize money she received as the 2009 laureate of the ULI J.C. Nichols Prize for Visionaries in Urban Development to help create the award.

"It has been my life's work to celebrate the essence of city life and to create great public open spaces," Burden says. "All successful planning comes down to the granular approach of how a building meets the street, how a street feels, how you feel walking in the city and coming to public spaces that are inviting and well used. Public space is why you stay in the city."

In 2011, the Kresge Foundation, the MetLife Foundation, and the ULI Foundation joined forces to sponsor the award, continuing the effort to celebrate and promote the development of vibrant and catalytic open spaces. Each year, the Urban Open Space Award is given to the individuals or organizations most responsible for the creation and regular upkeep of the winning projects, which are chosen by a renowned jury of multidisciplinary professionals.

From its inception, the award has been open to projects from the United States and Canada. This year, the award was expanded to accept and recognize international submissions. As the Urban Land Institute continues to strengthen its global mission, it is now more relevant than ever to share global best practices related to land use. Rapid urbanization and expansion in many countries have brought to the forefront the importance of urban open space, and we have seen many examples of exceptional open space initiatives worldwide that are worth recognizing and sharing.

To be eligible for the award, a project must:

■ be located in an urbanized area;

■ have been open to the public at least one year and no more than 15 years;

■ be predominantly outdoors and inviting to the public;

■ be a lively gathering place, providing abundant and varied seating, sun and shade, and trees and plantings, with attractions and features that offer many different ways for visitors to enjoy the space;

■ be used intensively on a daily basis and act as a destination for a broad spectrum of users throughout the year;

■ have a positive economic impact on its surroundings;

■ promote physical, social, and economic health of the larger community; and

■ provide lessons, strategies, and techniques that can be used or adapted in other communities.

This publication not only commemorates another extraordinary class of winners and finalists, but also aims to offer an overview of key issues raised in the context of urban development and open space. The goal in developing this framework is to continue supporting the discussion that is core to ULI's mission to create and sustain thriving communities.

The award winners and finalists through the years continue to demonstrate that an effort to transform the urban environment can catalyze blocks, neighborhoods—even entire downtowns. These projects are far more than amenities; they are models of ingenuity to create and sustain thriving communities.

Patrick L. Phillips
Global Chief Executive Officer
Urban Land Institute

Understanding the Value of Urban Open Space

Howard Kozloff

THE RECENT SURGE IN THE UNDERSTANDING of the value of open space is remaking the economic, social, and physical health of cities worldwide.

At their best, cities are complex organisms functioning as the result of many systems working in parallel. The physical, sociological, and economic processes—among many others—that keep cities humming are innumerable. A breakdown of one has cascading effects that can lead to the collapse of the others; but, similarly, the runaway success of another has the capacity to lift yet others to success, by whatever measure success in a city can be measured.

Enlightened and forward-looking planning has largely preserved open spaces—parks, plazas, waterfronts—for public access and set aside a lot of space for public use and activity. This alone, however, is not enough to create great urban gathering spaces. The physical components of a city include the streets, buildings, and sidewalks within and around which urban denizens function day to day. Parks and open spaces provide the "lungs of the city," a term credited to the great landscape architect Frederic Law Olmsted, who, along with his partner, Calvert Vaux, conceived of the expansion design of New York City's Central Park, which originally opened in 1857.

Olmsted and Vaux won a competition to expand the park in 1858 from 778 acres (315 ha) to 838 acres (339 ha). By 1873, construction on Central Park was completed, and it remains the most-visited urban park in the United States by tourists, workers, and residents of the immediate neighborhoods bordering the park, as well as by others from throughout the region. Though a significant component of the physical construct of New York City, Central Park plays a pivotal role in the socioeconomic well-being of the city as well, opening its gates to people from all economic and social classes.

Jake Watkins, senior associate at Roger Ferris + Partners Architects in Westport, Connecticut, notes that "parks hold a resource critical to any urban landscape. In both the largest and the smallest cities, parks have historically provided needed space for recreation, social gatherings, and a general reprieve from the built environment. Holding a vision of how parks can be planned and used within the fabric of a city has created some of the most memorable urban moments of several of the greatest cities."

Facing page: Historic urban open spaces such as Central Park in New York or the Champs-Elysées in Paris have become iconic references to articulate urban living. They continue to offer opportunities for flexible programming and design that engage communities and drive development.

UWE KEMPA, THE GATES, 2005

FRÉDÉRIC BISSON, LIGHTING AT L'AVENUE DES CHAMPS-ELYSÉES, 2013

Parks also carry the flag for open space as a transformative brand; in other words, Central Park as a name carries value in the city, most markedly demonstrated by the high-end apartments and offices ringing its exterior. Such famed buildings as the Dakota and, more recently, 15 Central Park West, a 202-unit condominium tower completed in 2008 by Zeckendorf Development at a cost of $950 million, derive their immense value from their proximity to the park.

Similarly, the 2010 opening of One Bryant Park, developed by the Durst Organization for anchor tenant Bank of America, signaled the pinnacle of urban open space. The $1 billion tower—a model of green architecture—capitalized on the growth in popularity of Bryant Park and cemented the Bryant Park submarket as among the most expensive in the city. The park itself is the product of an ongoing 30-year-plus effort that transformed Bryant Park into one of the most densely visited parks in the world through an innovative public/private partnership between the New York City Department of Parks and Recreation and the nonprofit Bryant Park Restoration Corporation.

Central Park and Bryant Park are two of the better-known examples of urban open space as a brand to drive positive economic impacts on their surroundings. Activity at the front door of a property—regardless of property type—affects real estate value. Oftentimes, what occurs on a day-to-day basis in the spaces between buildings determines desirability and, thus, value more so than the property itself. Take, for example, Santa Monica's Third Street Promenade or Paris's Champs-Elysées. Successful urban open spaces concomitantly promote physical, social, and economic well-being through intensive daily use by a variety of users throughout the year.

Tiffany Beamer, partner in the Los Angeles office of OLIN (designer of the 2015 ULI Urban Open Space Award finalist Washington Canal Park), lauds the sometimes-underappreciated effects of open space on community cohesiveness. "Our urban open spaces are the glue that holds our communities together—physically, psychologically, and socially. They are often taken for granted, as the absence of a building may translate into an absence of awareness of design, of place, of stewardship." Beamer continues, "What we know to be true is that the balance of great architecture and thoughtful landscape architecture—each supporting and feeding the other—is what makes our cities sing."

This variety of users, set against a backdrop of programming and design features singularly focused on usability, creates a sociological benefit to users and observers, and spawns a microeconomy to the benefit of surrounding property owners and businesses. When urban open spaces attract large numbers of visitors on a daily basis, when no special events are planned, they have become indelible and irreplaceable components of a neighborhood.

William H. Whyte, whose book *The Social Life of Small Urban Spaces* brought the sociology of urban open space to the forefront of urban parks discussions, noted, "A good plaza starts at the street corner. If it's a busy corner, it has a brisk social life of its own. People will not just be waiting there for the light to

Facing page: The multiyear effort to rejuvenate Bryant Park has positioned the park as a key reference for urban regeneration and downtown reactivation. High attention to detail and dedicated programming ensure its viability, which also results in high volumes of people using the space on regular, nonevent days. The park has featured prominently in the emergence of a more welcoming New York City. But often lost in the accolades is the tremendous effect the rejuvenated park has had on the real estate submarket.

change. Some will be fixed in conversation; others in some phase of a prolonged goodbye. If there's a vendor at the corner, people will cluster around him, and there will be considerable two-way traffic back and forth between plaza and corner." In other words, parks are not inward facing, but rather embrace the neighborhood by pulling people in and letting the activity of the park filter out to city streets.

Because of the considerable—if not critical—sociological components of successful urban open space, innovative partnerships are often spawned, while other times public entities have the in-house know-how and ingenuity to create great public destinations. The Myriad Gardens Foundation of Oklahoma City, the nonprofit organization overseeing the Myriad Botanical Gardens, provided capital and operating funds for the Office of James Burnett's Myriad Botanical Gardens renovation, which has a permanent fund that is managed by the Oklahoma City Community Foundation. And Washington Canal Park in Washington,

D.C.—an OLIN- and STUDIOS Architecture–designed park—is managed through the nonprofit Canal Park Development Association Inc. (CPDA). Tasked with promoting, designing, building, and maintaining the park, CPDA includes representation from the public sector (the D.C. Housing Authority and D.C. Ward 6), the private development sector (W.C. Smith and JBG), and another nonprofit entity (Capital Riverfront Business Improvement District).

Public sector–driven urban open spaces are no less successful. For example, Singapore's Urban Redevelopment Authority is both owner and designer of Marina Bay. The city of Chicago oversaw the development of Millennium Park, despite the inclusion of multiple designers and a complex and widely ambitious construction endeavor. Having been in operation for more than ten years now, Millennium Park has become a pivotal role model in this regard. In Santa Monica, California, Tongva Park and Ken Genser Square are managed by the city's community and cultural services and public works departments, transforming a parking lot into a community-sourced, James Corner Field Operations–designed park. And, similarly, retaining SWA Group as lead designer of Thousand Lantern Lake Park Systems in Guangdong, China, was the result of the Nanhai District Government's efforts.

In the realm of urban open space, for-profit, nonprofit, and government stakeholders each bring critical, and complementary, skill sets to their mutual goal of creating safe, attractive, and clean parks and plazas that drive economic development.

For-profit expertise includes negotiating experience—with vendors, consultants, and property owners, among others—to derive maximal value and operating efficiencies. Private sector management skills and the ability to execute in the absence of bureaucracy and red tape focus on a merit-based approach to performance metrics.

Nonprofit proficiency includes fundraising know-how critical to early-stage open space development, when a project vision is the only commodity and when momentum is only just materializing. Similarly, nonprofit groups can harness their community development experience to gather and reach consensus and bring in community programming partners to provide relevant and desirable park amenities, features, and programs.

Lastly, government and public sector involvement ensures a long-term view of public interest, providing a version of checks and balances to ensure that physical and social benefits are tantamount to financial gains for private interests, but still focused on economic development opportunities for the larger community. By bringing underused assets—for example, parks, plazas, and other open spaces—to the table, and by taking an entrepreneurial and opportunistic approach to planning, the public sector can set the table for the realization of transformative urban open space.

Even in cases where the public sector drives the development of a park, private sector buy-in is still essential in recognizing power to foster economic development. For this, "A critical component to the success of open space projects—especially in more challenging markets—is coordination [among] and buy-in from the for-profit, philanthropic, and public sectors; all three contribute in meaningful and necessary ways," says Ben Donsky, senior project manager for BRV Corp., which creates, redevelops, and operates

parks, public spaces, and neighborhood streetscapes on behalf of real estate developers, government agencies, and nonprofit organizations.

Design, of course, creates the physical embodiment of the results of partnerships and visions. Successful urban open spaces need comfortable and inviting gathering places that both anchor and bolster civic pride, and simultaneously provide backdrops for special events and day-to-day activity. According to Sean Baumes, project architect for Honolulu-based WCIT Architecture, "Open space in and of itself is not enough to be impactful. The elements that form that space need to be designed to engage the spirit of the community it serves and reflect the distinct character of the context with which it is placed. In that sense, it's less about the amount of money being spent or number of square feet needed and more about the thoughtfulness of the intervention."

Transformative urban open space does not come easily. While the end product makes it seem as though the initial idea was a given, such is rarely the case. The "transformative" moniker has to be earned through the initial vision of a champion, or champions, and implementation by a committed group of stakeholders. Initial public and private support has to be built, funding secured and sustained, spaces designed and programmed, and ongoing management put in place.

Targeted efforts are required to maintain success over an extended period of time, and those efforts are unique to individual spaces; no single solution exists. Leadership, both public and private, is critical in the face of a sometimes-vocal minority that will seek to derail a plan based on an aversion to change. Transformative urban open space takes the best of the public and private sectors—long-term vision, financial stability, opportunistic management, and entrepreneurial planning—to increase livability and enhance property values.

"Successful open spaces embrace and augment their frames," says OLIN's Beamer. "Whether they are gardens, piazzas, or something in between, at their best they provide a platform for social interaction and expression of the most democratic type. All the living systems of the city mix in these places—people and nature and culture. Ultimately, geometry falls away, and success is measured by the extent to which open space design supports and elevates those living systems."

Among the Urban Land Institute's priorities is the creation of resilient communities. Eliminating obsolete space and putting it to highest and best use creates thriving communities. Urban open space put to such use becomes truly transformative by acting as a catalyst for the elimination of obsolescence and the creation of social and economic benefits.

Cities are complex, with many competing needs across social, physical, and economic strata. Transformative urban open space has the unique capacity to provide gains across each. Long-term visions understand the socioeconomic benefits of urban open space, and the potential for economic development spin-off effects that can persist over time and accrue to stakeholders of all types.

HOWARD KOZLOFF is managing partner of Agora Partners, a real estate development, investment, and advisory firm based in Los Angeles.

Yards Park, Washington, D.C.

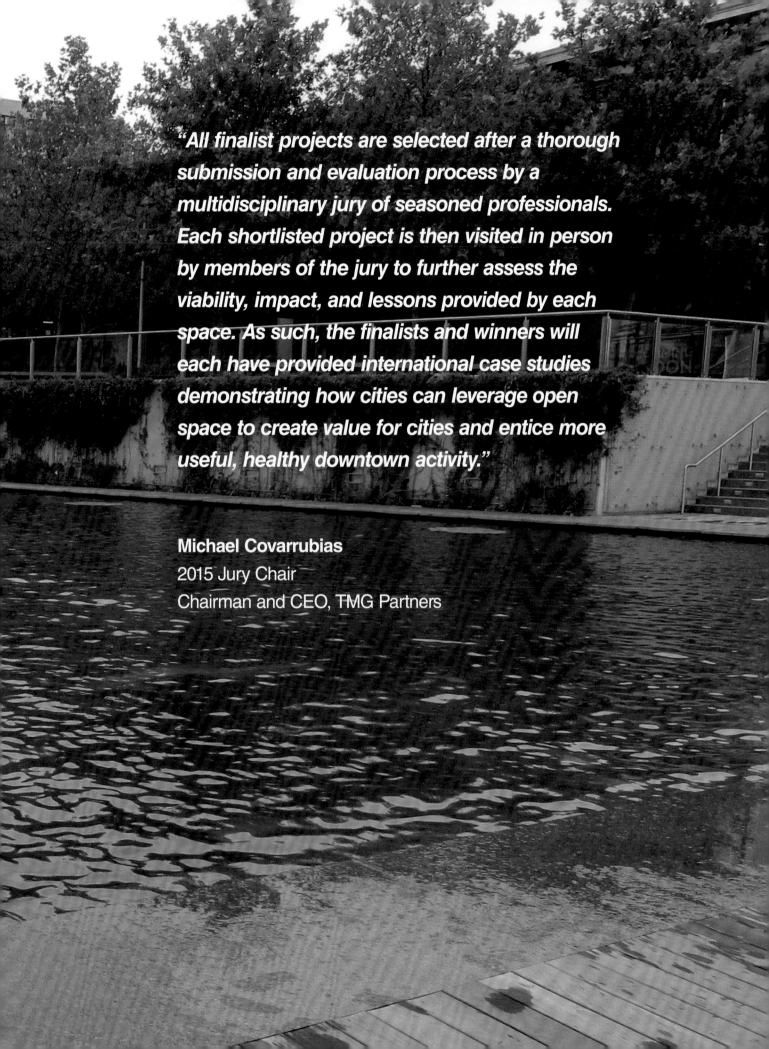

"All finalist projects are selected after a thorough submission and evaluation process by a multidisciplinary jury of seasoned professionals. Each shortlisted project is then visited in person by members of the jury to further assess the viability, impact, and lessons provided by each space. As such, the finalists and winners will each have provided international case studies demonstrating how cities can leverage open space to create value for cities and entice more useful, healthy downtown activity."

Michael Covarrubias
2015 Jury Chair
Chairman and CEO, TMG Partners

Myriad Botanical Gardens

Oklahoma City, Oklahoma, United States

Project owner: Myriad Botanical Gardens Foundation
Project designer: Office of James Burnett
Size: 15 acres (6 ha)
Project website: www.myriadgardens.org

BETWEEN 2009 AND 2011, THE CITY OF OKLAHOMA CITY, in coordination with the Myriad Botanical Gardens Foundation and the Alliance for Economic Development, invested more than $42 million to completely transform the Myriad Botanical Gardens. The goals for the project were to take the highly underused yet well-located 15-acre (6 ha) urban downtown garden and park site in the heart of the city that had fallen into disrepair and completely redesign all outdoor areas into a state-of-the-art, beautiful, green and highly active destination to improve the quality of life in Oklahoma City. The gardens have become an integral symbol of the new Oklahoma City and continue to drive the renaissance of the entire downtown. Today, acres of lush greenery grace the state's capital city.

The Myriad Botanical Gardens include a children's garden and playground, performance stages, a great lawn, interactive water features, an off-leash dog park, a seasonal ice rink, restaurants, multiple outdoor seating areas, landscapes filled with native plants, ornamental gardens, and more. Paths for walking and jogging serve as places for guests of all ages to find solitude in nature or connect with other community members. Park visitors can sit and enjoy the tropical scenery while listening to bubbling streams, and waterfalls blend into the sounds of the city. Should guests get hungry, the Park House restaurant is a welcoming indoor/outdoor, American contemporary restaurant with panoramic views of the Crystal Bridge and surrounding gardens.

Aerial view showing the great lawn and bandshell, water stage and lake, multiple walkways, and landscaped areas.

CARL SHORTT JR.

SHERIDAN STREET

OJB

Vision plan.

The 15,000-square-foot (1,400 sq m), 224-foot-long (68 m) Crystal Bridge Tropical Conservatory that stretches across the middle of the property is surrounded by a sunken lake, shrubs, flowers, and the outdoor water stage amphitheater. The living-plant museum features palm trees, tropical plants and flowers, waterfalls, and exotic animals. In addition to Crystal Bridge, several pieces of art are distributed throughout the gardens. Visitors can walk beneath the "Philodendron Dome" on the northwest side of the lake for views of iron vines woven into an iron-and-bronze dome. On the west side of the Myriad Botanical Gardens is a colorful kinetic wind sculpture titled *Land of the Brave and Free.* Two "spirit poles" commemorating 100 years of Oklahoma statehood grace the edge of the north fountain plaza. The gardens host many weddings year round in the different plazas, garden areas, and banquet halls that have views of the beautiful landscaping.

ZACH NASH

One of eight water features new to the Myriad Botanical Gardens, the Interactive Thunder Fountain attracts thousands of children and families who want to play and cool off during the warm summer months.

Thousands of visitors pack the Myriad Botanical Gardens during summer movie nights featuring a renovated great lawn, the band shell, a food truck area, picnic and al fresco dining areas, and safe lighting around the tree-lined perimeter.

The Myriad Botanical Gardens offer a variety of horticulture education programs for adults and children. Classes range from story reading to wreath-making workshops, with gardening day camps for adolescents during the summer. During the annual Oklahoma Gardening School, one of Myriad Botanical Gardens' signature events, acclaimed garden experts from the southern and southwestern United States share their advice for best trees, shrubs, and sustainable practices for the Oklahoma climate. Astronomy nights and adventure nights also engage younger populations in the outdoor space.

Visitors enjoy a walking tour along safe, lushly landscaped and lit walkways with winding streams and a rock waterfall.

Summers in the gardens are filled with a wide array of events and performances. Children's activities, such as crafts, snacks, and scavenger hunts, take place every weekday. Shakespeare fans can enjoy a series of outdoor plays at the water stage at dusk. If visitors are interested in moving to the beat, they can attend free dance lessons at Seasonal Plaza. Instructors teach salsa, western, swing dancing, and more. For those interested in a more meditative experience, the Myriad Botanical Gardens also host a weekly, all-levels yoga class at the pavilion. Afterward, guests can wander over to the Meinders Garden and Terrace for the Deep Roots Music Series, which features local and regional bands with a variety of "rootsy" genres. Country and blues listeners can bring their own chairs or blankets to the great lawn and band shell for the Sunday Twilight Concert Series. The Myriad Botanical Gardens offer something for everyone; speaker series, farm-to-table dinners, full-moon bike rides, movie nights, wine and painting, and even special events for pets are on their lineup. During the holiday season, visitors can stroll through the Winter Shoppes in the western plazas, take a ride on the carousel, or glide around the Devon ice rink.

The renovated outdoor water stage is the summer home to the nonprofit Oklahoma Shakespeare in the Park and hosts other performances, weddings, awards ceremonies, and demonstrations.

In order to maximize funding potential, a private/public partnership was formed so that the nonprofit Myriad Botanical Gardens Foundation could take on the management and direct earned revenue to ensure financial stability and raise funds needed to maintain the space throughout the year. The redesign of the site has attracted significant new developments near the perimeter of the park site, including a convention center, a hotel, several office buildings, and housing. Individual and family memberships, along with entrance fees and donations, help cover operational costs of the gardens. The gardens now attracts more than 1 million people per year with year-round activities and events for diverse audiences.

Thousand Lantern Park System

Foshan, Guangdong, China

Project owner: Nanhai District Government
Designer: SWA Group et al.
Size: 286 acres (116 ha)

LOCATED IN THE NEWLY ESTABLISHED district of Nanhai, the 286-acre (116 ha) Thousand Lantern Lake Park System provides a continuous urban corridor for the surrounding neighborhood. It consists of a commercial precinct, hotels, public parks, civic buildings, streetscapes, and a museum arranged around a series of lakes and waterways. The latter act as the connecting elements within the larger site and provide

The steps down to the lake at Citizen's Plaza are a popular spot for gathering and informal leisure activities.

TOM FOX, SWA GROUP

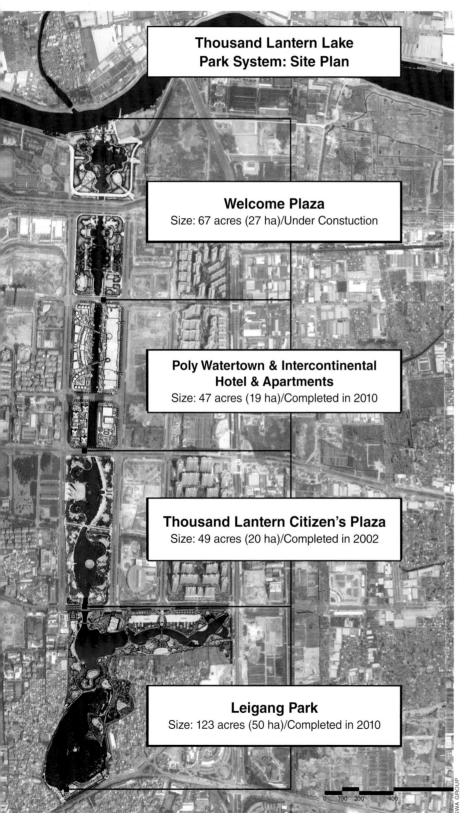

Thousand Lantern Lake Park System: Site Plan

Welcome Plaza
Size: 67 acres (27 ha)/Under Constuction

Poly Watertown & Intercontinental Hotel & Apartments
Size: 47 acres (19 ha)/Completed in 2010

Thousand Lantern Citizen's Plaza
Size: 49 acres (20 ha)/Completed in 2002

Leigang Park
Size: 123 acres (50 ha)/Completed in 2010

SWA GROUP

transportation networks that run through the entire park. The entire green, mixed-use corridor brings energy and liveliness to the city.

Formerly known as the South Sea Welcome Plaza, the Thousand Lantern Lake Park System represents a defining infrastructural success that has been integral to Nanhai's strategic plan for urban transformation over the past 15 years. According to the Foshan municipal government's work plan, this municipal park project has been included in the "Foshan three-year action plan to upgrade" project to be implemented in several phases. The Nanhai District exemplifies a people-oriented approach to urban development and provides creative solutions for attracting people to its newly constructed Guangdong Financial High-tech Industrial Zone. The park designers, SWA Group, structured the development around a north–south axis in order to honor *feng shui*. The development solves one of the greatest challenges that similar third-tier Chinese cities face: how to retain a community's vitality while the city upgrades its industrial structure to modern functionality, including a redefined spatial layout.

While many new cities of its kind suffer from being "empty towns," Nanhai attracts investors, new residents, and tourists for its celebrated Thousand Lantern Lake Park, now synonymous with the city's identity. The project incorporates a large municipal park, a forest landscape that includes built structures, large bodies of water, spacious green areas, and a large underground parking garage. Sited on land reclaimed from old industrial uses, the park system exhibits "big water" features that connect all new city blocks with a system of lakes, grand canals, and water alleys. It provides

The Thousand Lantern Lake Park System site plan and surrounding city.

Left: Designed to transition from day to night, the so-called City of Lights Thousand Lantern Lake Park features signature lighting designs at Culture Plaza that function as beacons in the dark.

Below: Historic elements honoring Nanhai's water town culture, including structures such as this existing bridge, are integrated into the new park layout.

TOM FOX, SWA GROUP

an active and passive waterfront for development properties as well as important drainage infrastructure. The centerpiece of the park, the 49-acre (20 ha) Citizen's Plaza on Thousand Lantern Lake, provides an active public gathering space that transitions from day to night with unique streetscape and lighting elements.

The 123-acre (50 ha) Leigang Park is named for the city's most prominent hill, around which it is situated; the peak operates as a landmark and orientation device for visitors within the park. Existing trees were preserved during development and integrated into the present design. Grand arcades throughout the park provide shade and seating for visitors, and classical tea pavilions are surrounded by waterways.

TOM FOX, SWA GROUP

As the core piece of this public open space, Thousand Lantern Lake has become the primary destination for recreation, events, and retail in the region, displaying the lively energy that contributes a significant competitive edge to the city's growth and value generation.

Marina Bay

Singapore

Project owner/designer: Urban Redevelopment Authority, Singapore
Size: 140 acres (56.2 ha)
Project website: www.marina-bay.sg

LOCATED AT THE HEART OF SINGAPORE'S CITY CENTER, against the backdrop of its signature skyline, Marina Bay presents an exciting array of opportunities for living, working, and playing. A successful example of Singapore's long-term planning, the larger Marina Bay area was progressively reclaimed over a 40-year period starting in the 1970s. The central business district was seamlessly extended, and a new city center was created around an urban waterfront. This development aligns with Singapore's plan for continued growth as a business and financial hub by raising the city-state's international profile while stimulating growth and investment.

Aerial view of the waterfront promenade around Marina Bay.

The Helix is an iconic pedestrian bridge built to connect the Bayfront and Marina Centre areas.

Today, Marina Bay has been transformed into a vibrant precinct with a mix of commercial, residential, hotel, and entertainment uses set amid well-landscaped public spaces and parks that serve as green lungs, tree-lined boulevards, and multiple open spaces. Marina Bay also boasts several event venues and gathering spaces for those living and working there. The Urban Redevelopment Authority (URA) realized its vision for an around-the-clock live/work/play environment in the heart of this global city.

Youth Olympic Park is Singapore's first art park, an open space with artworks and sculptures.

The waterfront promenade around the 120-acre (48 ha) body of water at Marina Bay is one of the key urban spaces within the city. It comprises a continuous 2.1-mile-long (3.5 km) waterfront promenade with two pedestrian bridges that link the adjacent developments, attractions, and event spaces. Marina Bay has the twin attributes of both water and greenery and is physically and visually connected to the adjacent open spaces, including Singapore's latest attraction, Gardens by the Bay, which has increased the urban space within the city by another 250 acres (100 ha). Along the waterfront and adjacent to open spaces, building heights are kept low to allow for optimal views of the city skyline. This creates a pedestrian-scaled area with a dynamic, "stepped-up" skyline profile in the distance. In addition, Lasalle College of the Arts gave the Marina Bay area a new twist with ten creatively designed public benches along the waterfront promenade. The project was headed up by the URA to encourage community members to draw inspiration from the bay.

Marina Bay is linked to an extensive transportation network. The development parcels at Marina Bay were planned based on a grid pattern that extends from the existing road network within Singapore's central business district. Visitors can easily access Marina Bay by way of multiple public transportation stations

Above left: The lower-level boardwalk allows for activities such as concerts to take place, bringing the community to the waterfront.

Above right: Breeze shelters along the upper-level promenade create pavilions for pedestrians to rest and gather.

and a system of cycling lanes. Marina Bay is also linked to the city by a vehicular bridge and the longest pedestrian bridge in Singapore. Pedestrians stroll through the signature double-helix design as they enter Marina Bay via the bridge.

The many venues at Marina Bay have become a focal point for events of all types, including large-scale international events. iLight Marina Bay, Asia's only sustainable light art festival, is slated to become an annual waterfront event. The site also hosted the opening and closing ceremonies of the inaugural 2010 Youth Olympic Games in a floating stadium on the bay. During the Formula One Singapore Grand Prix, spectators can watch competitors race around the Marina Bay Street Circuit from grandstands, from elevated trackside platforms, or on superscreens across the Circuit Park. The park covers an area of approximately 80 football fields, and the track cuts through areas of parkland filled with entertainment and activities in a tropical cityscape. A dazzling firework display choreographed to a musical score is the signature component of the Marina Bay Singapore New Year's Eve Countdown. For the 2014 event, live drumming accompanied the fireworks and buildings throughout the city were illuminated in Singapore's national colors.

Marina Bay has also attracted sporting events like the F1 Powerboat Race and the Oakley City Duathlon. These larger events have been complemented by regular community and sporting activities, such as weekend markets, outdoor concerts, mass walks, group runs, sailing, and canoeing programs that have attracted both locals and visitors, bringing buzz and vibrancy to the precinct throughout the year. The area is also home to the Marina Bay City Gallery, which offers information about the urban transformation of Marina Bay. Visitors can stop by the waterfront building to learn more about the latest developments, technological advancements, and events at Marina Bay. The gallery also operates complimentary guided tours and themed walking trails that provide facts about the development's architecture, public art, and heritage.

The next phase of development will include a mixed-use residential district, Marina South, next to Bay South Garden that is green, walkable, and bike-friendly. The Urban Redevelopment Authority is planning for the community to be threaded with streets, courtyards, and plazas that serve as outdoor living rooms for the community. Pedestrian walkways and cycling paths will connect residents to public transport nodes, with no station farther than a five-minute walk from any point in Marina South.

Millennium Park

Chicago, Illinois, United States

Project owner: City of Chicago
Designer: Edward Uhlir et al.
Size: 24.5 acres (10 ha)
Project website: www.millenniumparkfoundation.org

IN 1998, MAYOR RICHARD DALEY established a partnership with Chicago's philanthropic community called the Millennium Park Foundation (MPF), a 501c3 not-for-profit corporation, and together they produced Millennium Park. Mayor Daley sliced through a red ribbon and officially opened the park on July 16, 2004. More than ten years later, the inventive park is a boon for art, commerce, and the cityscape. A first-time visit to Chicago is not complete without a stop at Millennium Park.

Partial aerial view of opening day, July 15, 2004, with the first 300,000 visitors.

TERRY EVANS

Site plan of Millennium Park showing all the separate elements.

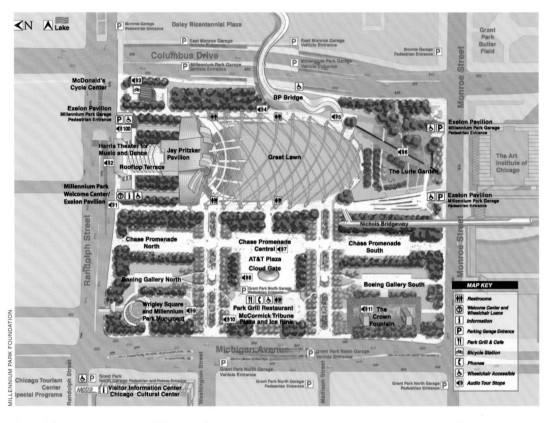

MILLENNIUM PARK FOUNDATION

Free concert at Frank Gehry's Pritzker Pavilion with its state-of-the-art sound system.

ED UHLIR

One might never guess that Millennium Park was once an industrial wasteland. Formerly a blighted lakefront area, the urban green space is now one of the most popular tourist destinations in the city. The project, located at the northwest corner of Grant Park, transformed 16.5 acres (6.7 ha) of rail lines, a surface parking lot, and another eight acres (3.2 ha) of shabby parkland built on top of a deteriorated underground garage into a unique outdoor cultural venue. It was built on top of two new underground parking garages, a commuter rail station, and a bus roadway, making it one of the largest public roof landscapes in the United States. Before the developers broke ground on this project, tourists rarely ventured south of the Michigan Avenue Bridge. Now, the area is teeming with visitors. Billions of dollars in real estate investment have revitalized the cityscape and bolstered the tax base, transforming the area into a must-see destination. Condominiums with views of the park cost an extra 29 percent, illustrating the Millennium Park ripple effect.

Millennium Park is a hub of activity nearly all year long. Visitors can stroll along the 925-foot-long (282 m) winding BP Bridge, commonly referred to as the Snake Bridge, to access the park from the Daley Bicentennial Plaza. Millennium Park is a place for Chicagoans and tourists alike to enjoy more than 80 free outdoor events every year, including weekly performances by the Grant Park Orchestra, popular concerts, exercise sessions, outdoor movies, performances by big-name artists like the Blue Man Group, artisan art fairs, blues festivals, jazz festivals, ballet and chamber music concerts at

the 1,500-seat Harris Theater for Music and Dance, and winter ice skating at the McCormick Tribune Ice Rink. During the summer months, events fill the Pritzker Pavilion nearly every night, with crowds of up to 11,000 people relaxing underneath dramatic ribbons of stainless steel suspended 40 feet (12 m) in the sky. The quiet 2.5-acre (1 ha) Lurie Garden, filled with mostly native plants, is lined by a 15-foot-high (4.5 m) "shoulder" hedge that represents Carl Sandburg's famous description of Chicago as the "city of the big shoulders." In addition, the Millennium Monument with stately Doric columns, a bike rental pavilion, the Park Grill restaurant, interactive public art, the Boeing Sculpture Galleries, and a world-class art museum next door are all packed into this walkable urban park area. No matter the season, Millennium Park offers activities for visitors of all ages.

Two art pieces within Millennium Park have received extraordinary public acceptance because they provide a community experience that is very interactive. On any given day, visitors can be seen photographing their reflections and the reflections of Chicago's storied skyline in Anish Kapoor's *Cloud Gate*, colloquially referred to as "the Bean." Jaume Plensa's Crown Fountain at the southwest corner of the park is a favorite spot for kids to play in the shallow water and for tourists to soak their tired feet. The two 50-foot (15 m) glass-block towers on either end of the shallow reflecting pool display the faces of 1,000 different Chicago residents. Periodically, the faces will open their mouths, which are perfectly aligned with spouts, and water spits out onto the plaza, delighting children and onlookers alike. Plensa claims the spouts are a reference to the traditional use of gargoyles, where faces of mythological beings were sculpted with open mouths to allow water to flow out. Both art pieces quickly established themselves as Chicago sculpture icons.

Millennium Park's many enhancements were funded by an extraordinary public/private partnership. The city's $270 million commitment was used to provide the park's infrastructure. The private sector raised $220 million from individuals, foundations, and corporations in order to provide park enhancements and establish an endowment of $25 million. Chicago's urban park is a sterling example of how bold investments in the public realm can pay dividends for decades to come. Millennium Park continues to spur private investment in condominium, office, and hotel construction near the park. The 11-year-old park's annual visitation has grown each year and now exceeds 5 million.

Many architects, landscape architects, and artists have contributed to the production of this new Chicago icon including McDonough Associates, Gehry Partners, Hammond Beeby Rupert Ainge, Renzo Piano Building Workshop, GGN, OWP/P, SOM, Terry Guen Design, Harley Ellis Devereaux, and Muller and Muller.

The Crown Fountain reflecting pool has become Chicago's free water theme park.

MARK SEXTON

Cloud Gate at night reflecting Michigan Avenue's historic street wall.

LUCAS COWAN

The re-creation of the 1918 Historic Peristyle provides a surface to acknowledge the 115 founders of Millennium Park.

ED UHLIR

Tongva Park and Ken Genser Square

Santa Monica, California, United States

Owner: City of Santa Monica
Designer: James Corner Field Operations
Size: 7.4 acres (3 ha)
Project website: tongvapark.squarespace.com

BUILT ON THE SITE PREVIOUSLY OCCUPIED by the Rand Corporation's headquarters and more recently a surface parking lot, Tongva Park and Ken Genser Square—once collectively known as the Civic Center Parks—encompass 7.4 acres (3 ha) in the heart of Santa Monica. The completion of these parks in 2014 represents the first step toward completing a plan for the 67-acre (27 ha) civic center area, which reenvisioned the area as a vibrant neighborhood with improved linkages to the Santa Monica Pier, Palisades Park, downtown Santa Monica, and Santa Monica State Beach.

Tongva Park and Ken Genser Square embody a new type of urban landscape that is active, innovative, resource-conscious, and natural. Shaped by extensive public participation, the design creates a contemporary and transformative series of gardens and active spaces that symbolically redefine and interconnect the center of Santa Monica. Tongva Park, named after the indigenous people who have lived in the Los Angeles area for thousands of years, forms a pedestrian and cultural corridor linking City Hall with surrounding commercial and recreational areas. With seven different entrances, the park is very open and integrates seamlessly into the fabric of the surrounding area.

Situated between City Hall and Ocean Avenue, park paths aspire to reach beyond the project boundary. They connect the civic campus with Santa Monica's active urban core and views of the city's defining landscape features beyond—the ocean and mountains.

STEVE PROEHL

The park's paths and mounds evoke the indigenous *arroyo* landscapes so typical of southern California. The design features dramatically rising and falling hills, which are inspired by washes and ravines that once occupied the site. Furniture elements are integrated into many of the park's topographical features.

JAMES CORNER FIELD OPERATIONS

Inspired by the southern California *arroyo* landscape of washes and ravines that once defined the site, a series of braided pathways appear to organically emerge from the footsteps of City Hall and extend west into Ken Genser Square, named after a long-serving councilmember and mayor of Santa Monica. The paths help weave the park into the fabric of the city. Though much smaller and more formal than its neighboring green spaces, the square is more than just a space to pass through when going to City Hall for permits and business licenses; seating areas and a water feature make it a great place to sit and have lunch or to enjoy the sunshine. The square serves as the focus for community gatherings and civic events and has become the "democratic space" symbolic of Santa Monica's city government and community dialogue.

Dramatic rising and falling topography reinforces the fluid pathway system and organizes the site into four thematic hilltop areas, each calibrated to a different primary use and experience. The park boasts hundreds of trees, a playground, public art, water features, and observation decks that offer views of the Pacific Ocean. Water elements are poetically linked by a single runnel that flows downhill to the ocean. Their volume and presence increase the closer they get to the ocean. Alcoves are carved into Tongva Park's

TIM STREET PORTER

Above: Chicago artist Iñigo Manglano-Ovalle's *Weather Field* is centrally situated in Tongva Park. A focal point, the sculpture is a grid of 49 telescoping stainless-steel poles, approximately 20 feet (6 m) high. Each is topped with a weather vane and anemometer, a spinning device for measuring wind speed.

Left: Overlooks fabricated from plasma-cut plate steel create a contemporary and striking park edge. They are as much about outward view as windows into the park, enticing passersby to enter the site.

Right: Observation Hill, which reaches a height of 18 feet (5.5 m), creates a dramatic platform from which one can take in views of the ocean and pier. It also serves to buffer noise pollution from Ocean Avenue, creating a quiet park interior.

TIM STREET PORTER

TIM STREET PORTER

Above: Seating terraces shaded by strawberry trees compose Gathering Hill, which is the social and civic heart of the park. The seating terraces function well for casual gatherings as well as for formal events such as Santa Monica's Jazz on the Lawn.

hillsides to create interior garden bays with seating for contemplation or exterior bays with bike racks and social seating for community comings and goings.

Landscape architect James Corner Field Operations, the group behind the design of the elevated High Line in New York City, designed Tongva Park and Ken Genser Square to act as a gateway into downtown Santa Monica, a community destination, and a city landmark. The project architect designed the park's comfort station as a grotto embedded in the rolling landscape. Large light tubes illuminate the "nonbuilding" facility, which complements art by Iñigo Manglano-Ovalle as well as majestic outlook viewing structures that provide views of the Pacific Ocean. The park plays an important cultural role within the community, providing an informal place for play, picnicking, strolling, jogging, sitting, and viewing. The bike and pedestrian paths create a series of physical linkages that unifies the open spaces, which also feature public art, horticultural exhibits, and commemorative elements.

Tongva Park offers a selection of free cultural events. Parents can bring their children to the park every Saturday from April through October for activities like hula-hooping workshops and puppetry performances. The "Tongva after Dark" series brings an array of live performances to the outdoor space during summer months. Past performances include South American cumbia band Buyepongo, dancer Holly Rothschild, and a hip-hop dance class led by Antics, a Los Angeles theater company. Display gardens, intimate alcoves, a play space for children, and a large, grassy open space on a hill all provide spaces for the community to come together. The events, in addition to the beautifully landscaped scenery, draw community members and visitors from outside the neighborhood to Tongva Park and Ken Genser Square. These urban open spaces exemplify the power of urban parks to build community and make cities sustainable and vibrant.

As a whole, the project offers a new model of sustainability for similarly scaled projects, one that carefully balances environmental and cultural considerations. From abandoned parking lots to the largest-scale Mediterranean meadow garden of its complexity in a public space, Tongva Park and Ken Genser Square have restored valuable ecosystem services and social vitality to a once derelict and degraded urban site.

Washington Canal Park

Washington, D.C., United States

Owner: Canal Park Development Association Inc.
Designer: OLIN and STUDIOS Architecture, dcpc
Size: 3 acres (1.2 ha)
Project website: www.canalparkdc.org

ONE OF THE FIRST PARKS BUILT as part of the District of Columbia's Anacostia Waterfront Initiative, Canal Park presents a model of sustainability, attaining both Sustainable Sites Initiative (SITES) and Leadership in Energy and Environmental Design (LEED) Gold certifications. The public/private partnership that was established in order to design, fund, and develop the project allowed for neighborhood-scale impact. The park has quickly established itself as a social gathering place and an economic trigger for the surrounding neighborhood.

As part of the District's Anacostia Waterfront Initiative, this three-block urban park sits in southeastern D.C., working as an economic trigger for the surrounding neighborhood.

Located on three acres (1.2 ha) of a former brownfield parking lot for district school buses, this three-block-long park is sited along the historic former Washington Canal system. Inspired by the site's 19th-century waterfront heritage, the design evokes the history of the space with a linear rain garden and three pavilions reminiscent of floating barges. In collaboration with OLIN, STUDIOS Architecture designed one pavilion to

OLIN / KARL-RAINER BLUMENTHAL

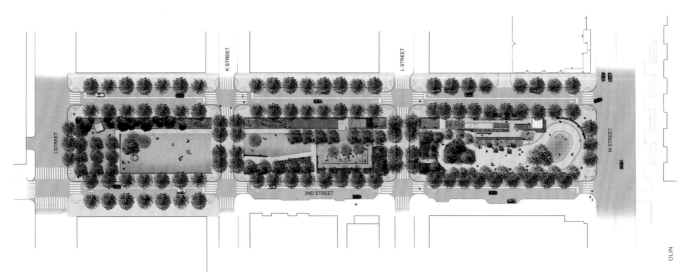

Above: Resting upon a three-acre (1.2 ha) commons, Washington Canal Park sits just a few blocks north of Nationals Park and the Anacostia River in Washington, D.C.

Below: In the winter months, the fountain is replaced with an ice-skating loop, recalling the tradition of skating on frozen canals.

host a café, while a second pavilion serves as a stage and a third offers storage for park amenities. Custom David Hess sculptures are located on each of the city blocks.

The park designers incorporated a diversity of activities and places that appeal to a wide range of people. In the warmer weather, the park hosts a farmers market, movie nights, and lunchtime concerts. The northern block is the most passive and serene, with a bosquet of trees leading to an expanse of grass. The middle block mixes pastoral spaces with active ones, like the fountain and floating stage pavilion. The southernmost block is the busiest, with a 250-foot-long (m) ice-skating loop that defaults to a gathering space in warmer seasons, and a 4,000-square-foot (372 sq m) pavilion that houses the Park Tavern restaurant, restrooms, and a skate-rental booth. While space is limited by the surrounding urban density, the project is a model for efficient, dense growth in D.C.'s rapidly developing Southeast quadrant.

The two streets that bisect the park were designed as "tabletop streets," meaning the street surface ramps up to meet the grade of the adjacent sidewalks, creating a flush transition between the street and sidewalk. The paving units used throughout the park continue across the street surface, creating an uninterrupted surface treatment for the full length of the park. These streets and the streets adjacent to the park were narrowed, indicating to drivers that they are in or near the park, slowing traffic.

Collaboration with the Washington, D.C., Department of the Environment (DDOE) led to progressive water management policy. The DDOE considers Canal Park a "demonstration project." The general schematic, the environmental assessment, and the maintenance covenant will be used as models for future projects with similar green infrastructure goals. The linear rain garden, the park's focal point, functions as an integrated stormwater system that is estimated to save the city 1.5 million gallons (5.7 million liters) of potable water per year. With the rain

Left: Custom David Hess stainless-steel sculptures are located on each of the city blocks, adding to the aesthetic unity of the park and designed for interactive play, while the great lawn offers a flexible space within the park for movies, concerts, and play.

Below: The interactive jet fountain, shade trees, and multilevel pavilion with an indoor café and outdoor dining area all sit on the south block of the park. The custom-designed ribbon bench wraps the edge of the fountain and is conducive to many different configurations and spontaneous play.

garden and 80,000 gallons (303,000 liters) of underground water storage capacity, almost all of the stormwater runoff generated by the park is captured, treated on site, and reused, satisfying up to 95 percent of the park's water needs for irrigation, building use, fountains, toilet flushing, and the ice rink.

Twenty-eight geothermal wells beneath the ice rink provide an efficient energy supply for utilities, which are estimated to reduce Canal Park's overall energy usage by 37 percent. Other sustainable design elements in Canal Park include dark-sky lighting elements, high-albedo paving, traffic-calming strategies, native and adapted vegetation, and site elements that encourage sustainable practices, such as electric car–charging stations, bicycle racks, and recycling bins.

The Capitol Riverfront Business Improvement District (BID) and its "Clean Team" are responsible for maintaining Canal Park. Revenues generated by the BID, by the on-site restaurant, and by the rental of skates at the park's winter ice-skating rink are appropriated to account for the site's maintenance and programming needs.

Canal Park provides a green pedestrian link between Capitol Hill and the Anacostia River, and it is a centerpiece for nearly 10,000 office workers and 2,000 new mixed market-rate and affordable housing units, which replaced 700 public housing units from across the District as part of the Arthur Capper-Carrollsburg

revitalization. Prior to park construction, the neighborhood had few amenities. According to surveys administered by the Capitol Riverfront Business Improvement District, the percentage of residents who view the neighborhood as "clean and safe" has gone from 30 six years ago to 90 today. Canal Park uses public open space and green infrastructure as an economic driver and acts as a catalyst for the revitalization of the Near Southeast neighborhood.

Above: The middle block pavilion doubles as a stage for children's music and theater and appears to float on a thin film of water, which creates a quiet area of play and respite for the park's youngest visitors.

Which Comes First, the Park or the People?

Peter Harnik

The logic and logistics of park-oriented development in urban areas.

Do you live within a half mile (0.8 km) of a park? Can you walk from your home to a park in ten minutes or less?

If you live in Boston, San Francisco, New York City, or Washington, D.C., the answer is almost certainly yes: nearly every resident in those cities has quick and easy access to some kind of public park space.

If you live in a more spread-out place, like Fort Worth, Texas; Columbus, Ohio; or Las Vegas, there is only about a 50/50 chance you can easily walk to your closest park. And things are more challenging in the sprawling giants like Oklahoma City, Memphis, and Indianapolis. In Houston, for example, more than 1.2 million people cannot get to any park, even a tot lot or a small urban square, without walking more than a half mile.

These facts, determined through mapping by the Trust for Public Land (TPL), demonstrate the need for many more parks for the increasingly urbanized U.S. population. Cities are rising to the challenge in creative ways, building deck parks over highways, converting asphalt schoolyards to after-school community parks, installing community gardens at abandoned properties, turning unused rail lines into linear parks, and more.

All these efforts help provide green space within a ten-minute walk for the millions of urban and suburban Americans who are too far from parks to derive the health, environmental, and rejuvenating benefits they

Spaces like the Columbus Commons and Scioto Mile are attracting residents and businesses back to the urban core. The spaces now bring over 1.5 million visitors annually, and have catalyzed more than $200 million in private investment in the RiverSouth District of Columbus, Ohio.

RANDALL SCHIEBER

offer. While a number of big-city mayors and even a governor have endorsed the goal of providing parks or other open spaces within a ten-minute walk of residents, adding enough parks to serve all 249 million people living in U.S. cities, suburbs, and urbanized areas—83 percent of the population—will be a challenge.

There is another, concurrent approach to providing Americans with a nearby park: bringing more dwellings to the periphery of existing parks to increase density on their edges. This is what TPL researcher Kyle Barnhart calls, "not only 'parks for people,' but also 'people for the parks.' "

The concept is parallel to the approach taken with transit. It is well established that the expense of building and operating transit lines can and should be earned back through the promotion of transit-oriented development—dense pockets of housing, commercial space, and retail development within 2,000 feet (610 m) of subway stations and major trolley and bus stops. Arlington, Virginia, for example, has won numerous awards—and achieved notable economic success—by closely tying compact residential and commercial redevelopment to six of its Metro stations.

The same logic can hold for park-oriented development. While studies by Smart Growth America and others show that transit is the strongest generator of demand for urban consolidation and density, parks can be high on that list, too. This has been shown in compact redevelopment in such places as Philadelphia (around Hawthorne Park), St. Paul, Minnesota (around Wacouta Commons), and Denver (along Commons and Confluence parks).

Surveys regularly find that people strongly desire greenery nearby, and they like providing a place for their children (and their dogs) to play. Even people who have no kids or animals and rarely go to a park significantly benefit from simply having a green view from a house or an apartment, as has been shown in research by Ming Kuo at the University of Illinois and others.

"The great thing about parks is that you can jump into them from just about anywhere," says Elizabeth Shreeve, a planner and a principal with SWA, a landscape architecture, planning, and design firm in Sausalito, California. "And it's particularly true for trails—long, thin parks that can have a few miles of edge and touch so many more communities."

Americans are not unified on the topic of density and parks, and that lack of consensus may be partly due to the many different mental pictures people have of both parks and cities.

Iconic photos from New York City and Chicago show massive walls of apartments facing Central Park and Lincoln Park, respectively. Philadelphia's Rittenhouse Square, San Francisco's Portsmouth Square, and Portland's new Jamison Square teem with activity nearly around the clock because of the large number of people living nearby. But that is not the rule. An ongoing study by the Rand Corporation is finding that some city parks around the nation are surprisingly lightly used, and part of the reason is that so few people live near them.

One dramatic case is Portland's 5,032-acre (2,036 ha) Forest Park, one of the largest city parks in the country, which has only 4,344 residents within a half mile (0.8 km) of its long boundary. It receives only about 500,000 visits per year, which sounds like a lot, but that works out to less than two persons per park acre every week.

In contrast, New York City's Riverside Park, much smaller at 330 acres (134 ha), serves more than 259,000 people within easy walking distance and receives about 3.5 million visits a year. Riverside Park and the adjacent Riverside Drive were specifically planned and designed in the 19th century as an amenity attraction for the development of scores of mansions, and later handsome apartment buildings, along the drive, and it worked.

In a few places, tall buildings could threaten the very parks they celebrate. In Manhattan, a recent spate of ultra-tall luxury condominium towers is casting shadows that reach into Central Park at certain hours during winter months. (These buildings do very little for urban density because their super-wealthy owners generally reside elsewhere most of the time.)

Parks in densely developed midtown areas of major cities might well require special zoning protection to avoid being cast in shade much of the year. San Francisco already has fought back with a stringent sunlight protection law that requires developers to replace every square foot of parkland that is newly shaded even one hour of the year.

One trend affecting densification around city parks involves the conversion of former manufacturing and office buildings to residential use. From Portland, Maine, to Portland, Oregon, and from Washington, D.C., to Seattle, Washington, business and industrial centers have been turned into or added to residential communities. As new residents move into the once-nearly abandoned historic downtown Los Angeles, how might that change demand for park amenities like playgrounds in Pershing Square or increase use of newly built Grand Park or Spring Street Park?

Small areas of pavement are transformed into usable urban open space, commonly known as parklets, in San Francisco's Pavement to Parks Program.

Finding the Revenue

Park-oriented development plays into two of today's realities: urbanites want high-quality parks nearby, and mayors need revenue to maintain the quality of those facilities. That revenue can come only from taxpayers, philanthropic donors, or people paying fees.

"In cities, density not only matters, it's crucial," says Mahlon "Sandy" Apgar IV, a real estate counselor and author. "Parks are one of the key features that can bring it about."

Apgar himself is living his aphorism. Beginning as an intern with legendary developer James Rouse, he has lived in London; Washington, D.C.; and Baltimore's suburbs. But after becoming empty nesters, Apgar and his wife, Anne, moved to Baltimore's Federal Hill neighborhood, which is anchored by the famed Inner Harbor and a historic park. There, they cofounded a park revitalization organization called South Harbor Renaissance.

Apgar is focusing his attention on finding a sustainable funding model to pay for better upkeep and management of that historic open space, Federal Hill Park. He thinks solutions could include market-based pricing for revenue-generating activities in the park,

a value-based local tax benefit for merchants who contribute in-kind support to the park, and a services-based assessment (such as those charged by private neighborhood associations) to pay for maintenance by the Waterfront Partnership, Baltimore's celebrated open-space management group.

"As Baltimore grapples with solutions to issues of employment, housing, and education, parks must be part of the mix as well to make it a healthful and beautiful city that unites and uplifts people," Apgar notes.

"Of course, conversations about density can be a flashpoint for a community," he adds. "People intuitively perceive the drawbacks more than the benefits. Most people don't link their neighborhood's density with the capacity and resources to improve their parks. So, that's what policy makers and officials themselves need to understand and then communicate to constituents."

PWL LANDSCAPE ARCHITECTURE

Opposition to greater building height or increased development density surrounding parks is often due to NIMBYism, he says. "And in older cities, it may be symptomatic of other issues confronting residents, such as antiquated infrastructure and inefficient public services despite high taxes."

Jamison Square, the first park added to the Pearl District in Portland, Oregon, is a model pocket park that, through a variety of inclusive features including a fountain, a boardwalk, and an outdoor gallery, enables a high level of use by the surrounding communities.

In the absence of lengthy conversations and public education, "battle lines are drawn between old-timers and newcomers who bring fresh ideas and energy to enliven community parks," Apgar says.

"Historically, inflexible zoning did not allow much room for experimentation. Now that's changing," he says. "The millennials' drive to the city and enthusiasm for shared space promotes higher-density urban design. Planned new communities have shown the way by integrating open space with denser mixed-use development and introducing flexibility to open-space zoning. And these innovations, thankfully, are moving from backroom deal making to more open neighborhood forums."

Baltimore has a triad of parks that illustrate the opportunities and challenges of the "people for the parks" concept.

Federal Hill is an eight-acre (3.3 ha) park in a crowded historic neighborhood. A few miles away, 135-acre (55 ha) Patterson Park, supported by a group called Friends of Patterson Park, is becoming steadily safer, more beautiful, and more active, adding significant value and appeal to its neighborhood; it seems likely that the housing market there would support replacement of some of the small surrounding rowhouses with apartment buildings.

But the story is different on the west side, where 700-acre (283 ha) Druid Hill Park was at one time the city's premier pleasure ground, surrounded by large apartment buildings and a dense fabric of fashionable brownstones. Because of severe neighborhood decline, the periphery today is a sad mixture of old buildings, vacant land, and a few new gated developments.

33

Zoning and Political Will

There is no one-zoning-fits-all solution to these myriad situations, nor a single best way of developing around parks. In some places, the housing demand simply does not exist; in others, there would be strong resistance from current residents to denser development. Apgar takes that concept further: he believes that large parks should not even be thought of as single entities. "One of Patterson Park's strengths is that it is large and diverse enough to have a mix of surrounding communities with different types of housing, different uses, and different markets," he says.

Rittenhouse Square in Philadelphia offers a diverse array of nearby amenities that, like Jane Jacobs pointed out in her seminal book *The Death and Life of Great American Cities,* generate an intricate range of uses and users of the park.

In all cases, local politicians and business leaders would have to understand that park-oriented development is economically beneficial to the city and environmentally beneficial to the surrounding region, just as is the case with transit-oriented development.

Clearly, with a few notable exceptions in places like New York City, many neighborhoods surrounding parks are far from being fully developed. In fact, with many urban communities in a state of almost continuous redevelopment flux, there is often room for gradual densification. A rough calculation shows that if the density around parks in all urban areas were slowly increased so that the half-mile-walk "catchment population" doubled from an average of about 1,850 people to 3,700, the number of new parks needed to provide the ten-minute walk to all city dwellers would be cut in half.

KEVIN BURKETT, 2010

This approach would not be easy. One person particularly aware of the importance of parks, but also of the challenge of density, is Jeremy Sharpe, vice president for community development for the Rancho Sahuarita master-planned community in Tucson, Arizona.

"The closer residents can be to a park, the better," Sharpe says. "A safe, well-maintained park is an amenity. We regularly survey our residents, and parks and trails continue to be the main reason people live in our community."

But density is a challenge, he says. "In principle, in gateway cities the park-oriented development idea makes sense. But in non–gateway cities like Tucson, the market doesn't demand that level of density," he says. "Yes, there is an increased interest in urbanity, especially by millennials. But according to two 2015 ULI studies, while 37 percent of millennials want to live in cities rather than suburbs or a small town (*America in 2015*), only 13 percent actually now live in or near downtowns (*Gen Y and Housing*). Most millennials want urban amenities in a suburban environment.

"Also, sometimes changes in the development process are difficult," Sharpe continues. "New ideas are often challenged, not because of the concept necessarily, but because there aren't existing principles to work under in the local market. Public planners have limits on what they're able to approve due to politics and zoning constraints. In our master-planned community, we've had to demonstrate some amenities and principles that were new and unfamiliar in our region."

Number of persons served within a half-mile of selected U.S. parks

Central Park, New York City	350,100
Riverside Park, New York City	259,000
Lincoln Park, Chicago	137,600
Golden Gate Park, San Francisco	104,600
Boedekker Park, San Francisco	39,300
Garfield Park, Chicago	22,200
Washington Park, Denver	11,700
Montclair Park, Denver	3,700

Source: Trust for Public Land.

Shreeve turns that thought around. "How about giving developers density bonuses for making improvements to existing parks?" she says. "Traditionally, in many places developers give land or money for new parks. But what if they also had the alternative of making our current parks better and allowing more people to live around them?"

Would this densification strategy cost more, or less, than simply buying more land? No one knows yet, but there is one major difference between the two approaches: buying the land requires public (and occasionally, private) money, whereas changing the urban form can be done largely through private financing. Small changes in zoning rules, incentives, or both can allow private developers to enter the market and assume the risk in return for likely profit.

Cities today are again ascendant, but they can also be difficult places to live without green space and other places providing respite. Creating new parks and working to fit more people around the edges of existing parks is a double-barreled way to get the most benefit to the largest number of people at a cost the nation can afford.

PETER HARNIK is director of the Center for City Park Excellence at the Trust for Public Land; he is author of *Urban Green: Innovative Parks for Resurgent Cities* (Island Press, 2010).

(Originally published in the September/October 2015 issue of *Urban Land*, pages 156–159.)

NATHAN WEBER

Campus Martius offers different programmable areas throughout the year. Since 2013, "the Beach" offers a summer-recreational area for downtown workers, families, children, and local organizations seven days a week, day and night. Ice skating occurs on a seasonal rink at the north lawn throughout the winter months. Special exhibitions are also possible on the rink with temporary seating that can accommodate up to 1,000 spectators. During the holiday season, a 60-foot (18 m) holiday tree tops the Woodward Fountain.

2010 Winner

Campus Martius Park, Detroit, Michigan
Project sponsor: Detroit 300 Conservancy
Designer: Rundell Ernstenberger Associates

Campus Martius Park has become the heart of downtown Detroit's development story and its signature public space. Surrounded by offices, residential space, and restaurants, it is a magnet for everyday visitors and high-profile events. Located on Detroit's main street, Woodward Avenue, the park has transformed the center of downtown from a recently desolate area to a beautiful oasis for everyday gathering. Campus Martius Park has exceeded all expectations. It is the most active year-round space in downtown Detroit, providing an outstanding environment for the more than 2 million annual visitors. Over $700 million of new development has occurred within a two-block radius of the park.

FINALISTS 2010

■ **Bremen Street Park, Boston, Massachusetts**
   Project sponsor and designer: Brown, Richardson & Rowe, Landscape Architects and Planners

■ **Falls Park on the Reedy, Greenville, South Carolina**
   Project sponsor: City of Greenville and Carolina Foothills Garden Club
   Designer: Andrea Mains; Tom Keiths

■ **Herald and Greeley Square Parks, New York, New York**
   Project sponsor: 34th Street Partnership
   Designer: 34th Street Partnership, Stantec

■ **Olympic Sculpture Park, Seattle, Washington**
   Project sponsor: Seattle Art Museum
   Designer: Weiss/Manfredi Architecture/Landscape/Urbanism

■ **Schenley Plaza, Pittsburgh, Pennsylvania**
   Project sponsor: Pittsburgh Parks Conservancy
   Designer: Sasaki Associates

2011 Winner

Citygarden, St. Louis, Missouri
Project sponsor: Gateway Foundation
Designer: Nelson Byrd Woltz Landscape Architects

Citygarden is a 2.9-acre (1.2 ha) richly landscaped sculpture garden and park that has altered the perception of the city's downtown and catalyzed nearby development. With a design that draws on St. Louis's chief natural feature—its rivers—Citygarden has succeeded in attracting a diverse public and creating an outdoor destination attraction and meeting place. Situated on two blocks of the Gateway Mall, the active sculpture garden has drawn visitors, residents, and workers back to the heart of St. Louis since opening in 2009.

FINALISTS 2011

■ **Discovery Green, Houston, Texas**
Project sponsor: Discovery Green Conservancy
Designer: Hargreaves Associates

■ **Jamison Square, Portland, Oregon**
Project sponsor and designer: Peter Walker and Partners
Landscape Architecture

■ **Raymond and Susan Brochstein Pavillion, Houston, Texas**
Project sponsor and designer: Thomas Phifer and Partners

■ **Simon and Helen Director Park, Portland, Oregon**
Project sponsor and designer: Zimmer Gunsul Frasca Architects LLP

Citygarden transformed the razed vacant old St. Louis Gateway Mall into an active park with 24 public sculptures carefully located in order not to overcrowd the space.

2012 Winner

Railroad Park, Birmingham, Alabama
Project sponsor and designer: Tom Leader Studio

Railroad Park occupies the historical seam created by a rail viaduct that bisects downtown Birmingham. The new topography integrates the train experience with a variety of new open-space activities that help organize and stimulate growth in the southern part of downtown while promoting connections north of the railroad. The park is the culmination of a long process of consultation and participation, including a 2002 ULI Advisory Services panel considering the entire downtown, followed by a new downtown master plan that identified key initiatives for growth and improvement. The resulting park is a model of integration, participation, and urban regeneration that will reward generations.

FINALISTS 2012

■ **Pier 25 at Tribeca Section of Hudson River Park, New York, New York**

Project sponsor and designer: Mathews Nielsen Landscape Architects P.C.

■ **Riverwalk Urban Waterfront, Calgary, Alberta, Canada**

Project sponsor and designer: Stantec Consulting Ltd.

■ **Tanner Springs Park, Portland, Oregon**

Project sponsor and designer: Atelier Dreiseitl GmbH

■ **The High Line, New York, New York**

Project sponsor and designer: James Corner Field Operations

The design of Railroad Park highlights the critical role that landscape architecture plays in the creation of reinvigorating open urban spaces, a practice that harmoniously engages art and social service. The park has become the most diversely used space by all area communities. Its establishment as a heavily used iconic space in the city and its beneficial engagement with surrounding areas by generating development reflect Railroad Park's success as an integral driver of urban living.

2013 Winners

The Parks and Waterfront at Southeast False Creek, Vancouver, British Columbia, Canada
Project owner: City of Vancouver
Designer: PWL Partnership Landscape Architects Inc.

Located on a previously industrialized 32-hectare (79 ac) waterfront site in Vancouver, the Parks and Waterfront at Southeast False Creek articulates the public realm for Vancouver's premier sustainable neighborhood. Through the introduction of restored natural environments into a highly urban community, the project exemplifies a new green infrastructure–based approach to creation of the public realm. The open spaces—composed of Hinge Park, Habitat Island, a 650-meter-long (2,132 ft) continuous waterfront park, and neighborhood streets—provide multiple and varied recreational opportunities while acting as kidneys for the neighborhood, cleansing stormwater runoff before it reaches the ocean.

PWL PARTNERSHIP LANDSCAPE ARCHITECTS INC.

PWL PARTNERSHIP LANDSCAPE ARCHITECTS INC.

Top: A new urban form emerged by marrying naturalized and built environments, creating a true sense of place in the Village.

Above: Hinge Park provides play, exploration, and adventure opportunities for residents and visitors to the community of all ages.

2013 Winners

The Yards Park, Washington, D.C.

Project owner: District of Columbia
Developer: Forest City
Designer: M. Paul Friedberg & Partners

The Yards Park highlights a regeneration effort that brings local communities and visitors to the Anacostia River while providing a transformative and vibrant public space that generates social, economic, and ecological value under an innovative public/private funding model.

Located near a Metrorail station along 1.5 miles (2.4 km) of Anacostia River frontage close to the U.S. Capitol, the space is the result of a pioneering public/private partnership among the U.S. General Services Administration (GSA), the District of Columbia, and Forest City Washington. Yards Park is the centerpiece of the Yards, Forest City Washington's 42-acre (17 ha) riverfront redevelopment of the Navy Yard Annex as a mixed-use area with 2,800 rental apartments, offices, shops, and restaurants.

FINALISTS 2013

■ **Brooklyn Bridge Park, New York, New York**
Project owner: Metro Nashville Parks and Recreation Department
Designer: Hargreaves Associates (Lead Design Consultant)

■ **Cumberland Park, Nashville, Tennessee**
Project owner: Metro Nashville Parks and Recreation Department
Designer: Hargreaves Associates (Lead Design Consultant)

■ **Wilmington Waterfront Park, Wilmington, California**
Project owner: Port of Los Angeles
Designer: Sasaki Associates Inc.

The Yards Park eschews monumental scale for a series of outdoor "rooms" organized around the central defining elements of water and topographic change. Its programming strategy includes both large-scale festivals and smaller gatherings. Yards Park serves as the cultural anchor to the Yards and the wider Capitol Riverfront area, reconnecting the city's grid to the water.

2014 Winner

Klyde Warren Park, Dallas, Texas
Owner: Woodall Rodgers Park Foundation
Designer: The Office of James Burnett–Landscape Design

Klyde Warren Park is Dallas's new town square that has literally and figuratively bridged the city's downtown cultural district with the burgeoning mixed-use neighborhoods to the north, reshaping the city and catalyzing economic development.

The park decks over the sunken Woodall Rodgers Freeway, which had been an imposing barrier between downtown and the densely populated Uptown neighborhood. Built with a combination of public and private funds, the park brings Dallasites together in new ways, with dozens of free activities and amenities to offer every week, from concerts and lectures to games and fitness classes, all within a five-acre (2 ha) model or development.

FINALISTS 2014

 **Columbus Commons and Scioto Mile, Columbus, Ohio**
Project owner: Scioto Mile: City of Columbus; Columbus Commons: Capitol South Community Urban Redevelopment Corporation

Designer: Scioto Mile: MKSK (formerly MSI); Columbus Commons: EDGE and Moody Nolan

Guthrie Green, Tulsa, Oklahoma
Owner: George Kaiser Family Foundation
Designer: John Wong

The Railyard Park + Plaza; Santa Fe, New Mexico
Owner: City of Santa Fe, New Mexico
Designer: Ken Smith and Frederic Schwartz

Washington Park; Cincinnati, Ohio
Owner: Cincinnati Park Board
Designer: Human Nature Inc.

Top: Built over an existing freeway, Klyde Warren Park provides a variety of flexible outdoor rooms that support a diverse range of free programmed activities. Since opening in October 2012, the park has been enthusiastically adopted by the citizens of Dallas.

Above: The groves of trees and arch structures at Klyde Warren Park establish a strong architectural rhythm through the park and buffer the interior of the park from the busy adjacent surface streets.

2015 Jury

Michael Covarrubias
Jury Chair
Chairman and CEO, TMG Partners
San Francisco, California, United States

Amanda Burden
Principal, Bloomberg Associates
New York, New York, United States

Jeff Barber
Principal and Managing Director, Gensler
Washington, D.C., United States

Terrall Budge
Principal/Owner, Loci
Salt Lake City, Utah, United States

Sujata S. Govada
Managing Director, UDP International
Hong Kong, China

Jason Hellendrung
Principal, Sasaki Associates
Watertown, Massachusetts, United States

Sophie Henley-Price
Principal, STUDIOS Architecture
Paris, France

Lance Josal
President and Chief Executive Officer, RTKL
Dallas, Texas, United States

Jeff Kingsbury
Managing Principal, Greenstreet Ltd.
Indianapolis, Indiana, United States

M. Leanne Lachman
President, Lachman Associates
New York, New York, United States

Jacinta McCann
Executive Vice President, AECOM
San Francisco, California, United States

Steve Navarro
Executive Vice President, CBRE
Greenville, South Carolina, United States

Trini M. Rodriguez
Principal, Parker Rodriguez Inc.
Alexandria, Virginia

About the Urban Land Institute

The mission of the Urban Land Institute is to provide leadership in the responsible use of land and in creating and sustaining thriving communities worldwide. ULI is committed to

- ▶ Bringing together leaders from across the fields of real estate and land use policy to exchange best practices and serve community needs;

- ▶ Fostering collaboration within and beyond ULI's membership through mentoring, dialogue, and problem solving;

- ▶ Exploring issues of urbanization, conservation, regeneration, land use, capital formation, and sustainable development;

- ▶ Advancing land use policies and design practices that respect the uniqueness of both built and natural environments;

- ▶ Sharing knowledge through education, applied research, publishing, and electronic media; and

- ▶ Sustaining a diverse global network of local practice and advisory efforts that address current and future challenges.

Established in 1936, the Institute today has more than 35,000 members, representing the entire spectrum of the land use and development disciplines. ULI relies heavily on the experience of its members. It is through member involvement and information resources that ULI has been able to set standards of excellence in development practice. The Institute has long been recognized as one of the world's most respected and widely quoted sources of objective information on urban planning, growth, and development.

Patrick L. Phillips
Global Chief Executive Officer
Urban Land Institute

ULI Project Staff

Kathleen Carey
Executive Vice President, Chief Content Officer

Daniel Lobo
Director, Awards

Kathryn Craig
Senior Associate

Steven Gu
Associate

Kelsey Padgham
Content and Leadership Intern

James Mulligan
Senior Editor

David James Rose
Editor/Manager

Betsy Van Buskirk
Creative Director

Anne Morgan
Graphic Designer

Craig Chapman
Senior Director, Publishing Operations

About the Kresge Foundation

The Kresge Foundation is a $3 billion private, national foundation headquartered in metropolitan Detroit, in the suburb community of Troy, that works to expand opportunities in America's cities through grantmaking and investing in arts and culture, education, the environment, health, human services, community development, and place-based efforts in Detroit. In 2013, the board of trustees approved 316 awards totaling $122 million; $128 million was paid out to grantees over the course of the year. In addition, the Foundation's Social Investment Practice made commitments totaling $16 million in 2013.

About MetLife Foundation

MetLife Foundation was created in 1976 to continue MetLife's long tradition of corporate contributions and community involvement. Today, the Foundation is dedicated to advancing financial inclusion, committing $200 million over the next five years to help build a secure future for individuals and communities around the world. The Foundation's vision for global financial inclusion is built on three powerful pillars: access and knowledge, access to services, and access to insights. MetLife Foundation has provided more than $530 million in grants and $100 million in program-related investments to nonprofit organizations since its inception.

About the ULI Foundation

The mission of the ULI Foundation is to serve as the philanthropic source for the Urban Land Institute. The Foundation's programs raise endowment funds, major gifts, and annual fund monies to support the key initiatives and priorities of the Institute. Philanthropic gifts from ULI members and other funding sources help ensure ULI's future and its mission of providing leadership in the responsible use of land and in creating and sustaining thriving communities worldwide.

ULI Foundation Staff

Patrick L. Phillips
President

David E. Howard
Executive Vice President

Corinne Abbott
Senior Vice President, Foundation Relations

Andrea Holthouser
Vice President, Individual Giving